SAGING -

How to Grow Older and Wiser

To Bob —
A young-at-heart soul!
Amitiés —
Joan

by

JOAN Z. SHORE

SAGING

Library of Congress Registration Number TXu-981-221
ISBN 0-8197-0715-5
© 2000, 2003 Third edition
Joan Z. Shore
GG/F Press - Paris, France

CONTENTS

PREFACE

No wise man ever wished to be younger. /Jonathan Swift

There's a difference between growing older and growing old.

We all grow older. From the moment we're born, our life's course is to grow older. We grow older relative to what we were, and who, after all, wants to remain an infant?

But many of us, most of us, also grow old. And "old" is not a relative value; it's an altered state which comes upon us slowly or swiftly, and which binds us, consciously or unconsciously, to an altered, limited mode of life. While growing older is a natural evolution, growing old implies a radical shift in our physical equilibrium, our mental outlook, and our emotional responses.

This is something we should start thinking about when we're still young, but of course we don't. Only when the first gray hairs appear or an illness strikes or a parent dies do we pay attention, and try feebly — or desperately — to put the past in its place and keep the future at bay .

This book is predicated on the premise that our life is shaped not merely by our upbringing, our genes, and our experiences, but most importantly by our attitudes. The same family nucleus will produce children of wildly differing characters — even identical twins will have different personalities — and we all know how common experiences in life will affect individuals in different ways. It is the attitudes we have learned and cultivated that ultimately determine whether our life is happy or unhappy, and whether we view ourselves as a success or a failure.

Many modern therapies try to help us do this, and this book by no means claims to be a substitute for these profound and often effective programs. But not everyone needs such intensive work to achieve a greater sense of pleasure and confidence and well-being. Attending a seminar, hearing a lecture, or reading a book can often jump-start a new train of thought, which leads to a new field of insight and action.

This is not simply a question of mind over matter, but of mind over mind. For by adopting and practicing certain attitudes or character traits (and discarding others), we may overcome the despair, the disappointments, the disillusion, the distress, and perhaps much of the disease that comes with age. Some of these suggestions may seem self-evident, even simplistic; some may sound strange or outrageous; and there are others which may occur to you, personally, which I have omitted. Add these to the list.

I don't discuss relationships in this book — love, sex, marriage, family, friendship — because the focus here is on the individual as a self-reliant unit. Of course, "no man is an island", and personal relationships are important: they are a mirror of ourselves and a training ground for our development, as well as an enhancement of our lives. But too often, we use other people as crutches, or substitutes, and as providers of the comfort and pleasure we cannot create ourselves. Before we can find harmony with another person, we have to find harmony within our own being.

Please remember that I coined the word "saging" from two nouns, Age and Sage, transforming them into an active verb. The idea is that we should not only age gracefully, but with intelligence, pride, and joy.

Whatever your age, it's not too late to start. And it's not too soon.

Joan Z. Shore
Ile St.-Louis, Paris

PART I

Chapter 1

INTRODUCTION

Man fools himself. He prays for a long life, and he fears an old age. /Chinese saying

The world is growing older, along with the people in it. The planet shows signs everywhere of environmental deterioration, of pollution, of waste and refuse, of the abuse and misuse of natural resources, of man-made disasters (from a pot-holed ozone layer to nuclear energy accidents to oil spills), of unbalanced distribution of populations (with unmanageable and unlivable mega-cities on every continent), and a rapidly shrinking gene bank as plant and animal species are carelessly and callously eliminated.

Certainly, humans have benefited to a huge degree from the world's devastating progress: science, medicine and economic conditions have lengthened our longevity and spared us much suffering. Yet there is, increasingly, deep concern about the diminished quality of life and the dreary prospects for the elderly. Is early retirement depriving us of years of personal productivity and fulfillment? Is "assisted living" merely a metaphor for isolation and abandonment? Are "senior communities" removing us from real life?

Curiously, at the same time, there is more and more talk of living longer and someday achieving immortality, using such fantastical technology as cryogenics and stem cell therapy. If aging is so onerous, and raises such difficult problems, why are we trying to prolong it?

Ironically, at the other end of the scale, we have been shortening childhood relentlessly, exposing children to adult violence and sex, dressing them up in designer clothes, and embellishing them with cosmetics and plastic surgery. Why do we put our young lives on fast forward, and then, at thirty or forty, try to push the "pause" button, and at sixty or seventy try pathetically to rewind? Of course, there are huge commercial and economic interests involved, with profits to be made, but there is also the subversive collective ego. (Some call it the *zeitgeist*, but I think it is something more pernicious than that, more pathological.) This collective ego sees childhood as a nuisance, adolescence as a trial, maturity as a necessary evil, and old age as a burden. It sees the ideal age as twenty to thirty: fresh out of college, working at an overpaid, fast-track job, with a strong, healthy and beautiful physique. Nice, but why rush to get there, why struggle to stay there, and why deny there are other interesting stages in life?

Clearly, the challenge is to find a new definition of life — a new perspective that doesn't see only highs and lows, like a topographical map, but which charts the journey with joy and excitement. Our life, in this sense, is a landscape, and there is as much beauty in the valleys and deserts as there is on the mountain peaks.

*   *   *

Even more weird than the talk of immortality is the new idea that age is a disease. I first encountered this preposterous notion at a public conference held in southern Florida. A newly-formed organization of anti-aging "experts" told an elderly and not-so-elderly audience that aging was an illness for which cures were being sought and found. (Among their simpler recommendations: melatonin and DHEA.) Another group of specialists, holding an anti-aging conference in Monte Carlo, warned that aging was becoming an "epidemic". Well, I suppose if you consider how many more people are reaching a ripe old age, then human longevity has indeed reached "epidemic" proportions! Are we unhappy about that?

To define aging as a disease is as absurd as saying that birth, puberty, menstruation, pregnancy, menopause, or the climactic are diseases. They are all natural processes of growth and change and in no way harmful to the individual's health.

The only time our well-being is perturbed or destabilized by a natural process or event is when we bring to it a negative attitude. This is also true of all external, "unnatural" events as well — people and happenings outside of us which impact our lives — but this is a much harder truth to accept. Yet by starting in a small, personal way to shift and monitor our attitudes toward ourselves and our life, we can gradually expand outwards, eventually encompassing our family, our friends, our community, and our world in a way of life — a way of being — that is joyful and liberating.

Chapter 2

SIMPLICITY

Everything should be made as simple as possible, but not simpler. /Albert Einstein

In many ways, simplicity is the simplest attitude to cultivate, which is why we can start with it. Yet it can be unsuspectingly difficult, too. Imagine a lifetime of accumulation: possessions, friends, documents, habits, obligations. Imagine deciding one day to pare it all down: where would you begin?

First of all, *why* would you begin? Why would you give up any portion of the stuff that defines and expresses your life? — things that serve as souvenirs, people who once were or might again be close to you, documents and files that might one day be needed, habits that help you get through the day thoughtlessly and easily, obligations you have kept and respected unquestioningly, perhaps even inherited from your parents. Like that old coat hanging for years in the closet, unworn, these are things that once were enjoyed and used, and that might still give a sense of comfort and security.

Sentiment and security have their place, but they are not enhanced by accumulation. In fact, they are probably diluted by it. Too much of anything obscures the value of the truly special *"objet rare"*. Too much stuff creates anxiety over maintaining it, insuring it, and just keeping track of it. Unexamined habits and routines create clutter, too — or perhaps a vacuum — leaving no room for better methods, new ideas, and novel experiences.

In physics, there is a law that complexity increases with development, or age. How true this is in our own lives. Up to a point, we can call it enrichment, but beyond a certain point it becomes useless multiplication. There is the spare hair dryer, the extra set of dishes, the shelves of once-read or never-read books, the shoeboxes full of unsorted photographs, the abandoned sports equipment, the rusted garden shears. . . . .

If complexity comes with age, then simplification may be a way to de-age. Look around and think seriously about all the excess baggage in your life: knick-knacks on the coffee table, gadgets in the kitchen, clothes in the closet. If you think it's wasteful just to throw things away, donate them instead to a charitable organization. The sense of freshness and spaciousness that comes with merely emptying and organizing one drawer will encourage you to continue: to an entire desk, to a closet, to a room.

Simplicity extends to activities, too. Taking a short walk along a favorite street instead of a long drive to a shopping mall; organizing an informal buffet dinner instead of a catered cocktail party; planning a visit to one foreign country, in depth, rather than a hectic tour of several . Even something as nerve-wracking and time-consuming as buying holiday gifts can be reduced to a simple system: a fine bottle of wine, an excellent box of chocolates, or a beautiful bouquet — for everyone!

Making lists can appear to simplify our life, but more often it becomes a way of stalling for time. Lists will be more effective if they are drawn up either by priority, with the most urgent items first and the rest in descending order; or by grouping items of the same nature, such as all the telephone calls, all the errands in a certain neighborhood, all the home-based tasks. Striking out what you've done, item by item, gives the same sense of satisfaction as cleaning out that drawer!

It doesn't take much work to figure out where your life is overgrown with stuff, but it takes enormous willpower to do something about it. Throwing out that old tennis racquet, that chipped vase, that duplicate copy of Fanny Farmer, that dubious African sculpture bought in the Paris flea market — these are acts of courage. Even more courageous is it to stop sending Christmas cards to people you never see (or maybe you should send them *only* to people you never see, and not to those you do!). It's also courageous to clean out the medicine cabinet, to give up the third car, and to decline two of the three invitations you have for the weekend.

Our lives are defined as much by what we reject as by

what we accept. Extremism, in either case, creates distortion and imbalance. In our Western world, especially, we have opted for profusion, confusing quantity with quality. We consume voraciously, amass indiscriminately, and gild all the lilies. . . . unnecessarily. A retreat now and then — a weekend alone, a day of music, an afternoon at a museum — can help clear the fog, but a real effort is needed to translate our good intentions into action, to bring a sense of restraint, balance and thrift into our lives.

Yes, thrift! The opposite of thrifty is, curiously, spendthrift, not extravagant. "Extravagant" can be quite wonderful: the extravagant gesture, the extravagant celebration. It belongs in the realm of the exceptional and unusual. Thrift, however, is the day-to-day balancing act, using analysis and discrimination. And it needn't be dreary. Deciding what to do and what not to do, what to keep in one's life and what to discard, what to pursue and what to drop, has a very positive aspect.

The hardest things to simplify in our life are the things we're not conscious of: the myriad obligations we've taken on, and the complicated habits we've acquired. Learning to say no can be a lifelong lesson, yet it becomes more and more necessary as we grow older. We recognize then that our time is precious, and our energy is lessening. In fact, we have a ready-made alibi, almost as pregnant women do!: "Oh dear, I'm just not feeling up to it."

But why even make this excuse? Evaluate what promises you really want to keep, which ones you have been bullied into, and which ones no longer give you pleasure or satisfaction. What obligations do you want to continue to honor? Which ones do you want to cut down on? Which ones do you want to cut out? Be ruthless! Babysitting grandchildren, selling church raffles, serving tea at community fund-raisers, should never become a deadly chore, where your help is taken for granted and your resentment eventually boils over. Conserve your energy for activities that don't sap your goodwill, but truly radiate it.

Habits and routines are the other area where we are largely unaware of our complex, constricting and often compulsive behavior. Sometimes, with life becoming ever more fragmented and specialized, we cannot avoid the rat race of multiple medical appointments, duplicate household services, numerous financial accounts, and incessant errands to run. Yet that makes it all the more imperative to try to rationalize and streamline our activities. This may mean giving up the individual shops and merchants and service providers we deal with and finding competent, one-stop, full-service establishments: the health club with a beauty salon and barber shop, the clinic with a full staff of specialists and specialized equipment, the firm that handles all home repairs, the institution that services all your financial needs. Of course, if you have a broad network of reliable personnel — people you can call at the drop of a hat and count on to get a quick response — then stay with them. They are saving you time and aggravation in the long run. But if your time is gobbled up with phone calls, appointments, and cross-town travel, think about consolidating your support structure.

The answers to these questions might help simplify your life quite profoundly. Or they may open you up to some interesting discoveries. That is what the next chapter is about.

Notes

Where is my life overgrown and cluttered?

_____

_____

_____

_____

What can I throw out or give away?

_____

_____

_____

_____

What am I doing that I don't want to do anymore?

_____

_____

_____

_____

Other thoughts:

_____

_____

_____

Chapter 3

CURIOSITY

*A generous and elevated mind is distinguished by nothing
more certainly than an eminent degree of curiosity.*
/Samuel Johnson

"Curiosity killed the cat, satisfaction brought it back".
As far as humans are concerned, curiosity will never
kill you. In fact, it will "bring you back" from boredom and
help you live more fully.

An uncurious mind is a closed mind, a dead mind. It is
hermetically sealed against new concepts, new ideas, new
knowledge, and, therefore, new experiences. Science tells
us that the mind is always working, even while we sleep,
but a closed mind is always *re*working — like a farmer tilling
the same plot of earth, over and over, and never sowing,
growing and reaping a harvest.

As young children, we possess a "natural" curiosity, for
we are fresh and new in the world and have a lot to learn.
Sometimes, tragically, those natural urges to explore are
suppressed by the adults around us: parents with too little

patience or humor or understanding to help and encourage us; teachers with too little time or imagination to indulge our experimentation. Even if we have the benefit of a curious childhood, at a somewhat later point in our lives we run into a wall of restriction and conformity. We learn "right ways" and "wrong ways" of doing things, "right" and "wrong" answers, "right" and "wrong" behavior. Much of this is necessary to ensure our social adaptation and academic success, but much of it stunts the development of our inner selves, our true individuality. The wall gets higher as we marry, get a job, have children of our own. Granted, there's a certain easiness in following the rules, and even a certain sense of security, but we have lost the sense of innovation and discovery.

Being curious doesn't necessarily mean you're a rebel or a social outcast. (Those categories of people are sometimes the most closed-minded and dogmatic types!) But it does mean you are ready and willing — and even amused — to question the status quo, to expand your knowledge and deepen your understanding, to try on new concepts and different ways of doing things. For our patterns of thought and action are so ingrained that most of the time we are completely unaware of them: reading the same newspaper every day, taking the same route to work, buying the same brand of coffee, using the same adjectives (great!, awful, incredible!, crazy, super!, dumb). We make up our minds months in advance how we're going to vote, conclude that all painting after Van Gogh is trash, believe that all foreigners are untrustworthy, and decide that green is unbecoming. But have we listened to the candidates?, visited art galleries?, made friends with "foreigners"?, tried wearing green? Probably not.

Curiosity can be delightfully shallow or stunningly deep. It can be spending half an hour in a bookstore, browsing around several shelves, or it can be signing up for a course in hatha yoga. It can be trying out a few new plants in the garden, a new recipe for fondue, or a new hair style. It could be tracing your family tree or researching the history of your community. When you have an open frame of mind, almost everything will grab your attention and spark questions.

One of the most endearing forms of curiosity is our curiosity toward others. Diana Vreeland, the iconic editor of Vogue, said that the thing that most interests people is people. I don't think she meant a prying, prurient interest, which is what we are exploiting today in our tabloids and glossies and personality-cult talk shows. Rather, there is the healthy human desire to make contact, to converse, to exchange, to apprehend, and the way we do this is by asking questions and listening. Curiosity prompts the question and listening — a disappearing talent in our world — delivers the answer. Few things crush communication as quickly as a barrage of questions fired by someone who isn't listening to the answers. The message is, "I'm not really interested". Curiosity without receptivity is merely a waste of time, and when another person is involved, it amounts to an insult. Curiosity about oneself can lead to important insights, which in turn could lead to positive changes in attitude and behavior. For example: Why do I get angry/resentful/fearful in certain situations? What childhood experiences do I remember that particularly affected me? Why am I reluctant to do certain things, and eager to do others? If the problems are truly serious, a professional therapist should be called on for help. But if you can tackle it alone, or with a trusted friend, you'll find a little self-analysis goes a long way. Only be careful not to get so self-obsessesed that you have no curiosity left for anything else!

Being curious, being open, being receptive, helps to keep your world fresh and interesting. But don't fake it! It won't work. (Admit that you don't really want to learn Spanish, but you'd love to learn more about Socratic philosophy.) Be sensible. (Try out the equipment at the local gym before you invest in a Nautillus.) Be realistic. (Don't take up a friend's dare to go surfing if you have chronic back pain.) Above all, be your curious, creative self and see it all as fun.

That takes us to the next chapter.

Notes

What sorts of things arouse my curiosity, grab my attention?

_____

_____

_____

What have I always wanted to learn or study?

_____

_____

_____

What do I have the least interest in, or curiosity about? Why?

_____

_____

_____

Other thoughts:

_____

_____

_____

Chapter 4

HUMOR

The young man who has not wept is a savage, and the old man who will not laugh is a fool.   /George Santayana

One of the worst things you can say to someone is that (s)he has no sense of humor.

Why is this remark so devastating? After all, you're not criticizing that person's intelligence, charm or competence.

Or are you?

When you really think about humor, it is much more than just the ability to tell a good joke, or to appreciate one. It is more than having a nice chuckle or a good belly-laugh from time to time.

Humor is an attitude, a point of view, that is often the result of that open mind we were discussing in the last chapter. Humor goes a step beyond curiosity, however, because it involves another degree of intelligence. For example, to see the humor in a situation, you have to recall other situations, or imagine other situations. Instead of merely viewing the present event in its fixed state, you're setting it in a new frame of reference. This can be done in the wink of an eye, or gradually over a period of time. What matters is that the situation (or the person, or the idea) is given a new context, a new spin.

Of course, this kind of thinking can also serve a serious end: it's a form of comparison and analysis. But most events in our lives do not (or should not) raise grave questions that demand grave analysis and grave answers. Most events in our lives are small and fleeting: an argument with the plumber, a traffic snarl, a lost telephone number, a malfunctioning VCR, a canceled engagement. This is when humor comes and saves the day, keeping the event in proper proportion and sparing us howls, haste and hysteria. Also hurt, hostility and hubris. And maybe a heart attack.

How do you develop a humoristic point of view? There are many ways, many approaches. The easiest (and maybe least funny, because it's so existential) is simply the French phrase: "C'est la vie". Say it with a shrug, as the French do, and with a smile (as they don't). Try translating it into any other language you know, even English. (A good Yiddish equivalent, I'm told, is "Azoi is de velt".)

Another approach is more cerebral. Think of all the other times you have faced that situation (you can surely remember some of them) and recall what happened. Was there a funny or ironic twist in the end? (The plumber apologized. The person whose number you lost called up the next day. The cancelled engagement allowed you to attend another, more interesting, event.) And if you can't recall any happy or funny ending, imagine one. (This traffic delay is making me so late I'll miss the boring opening speeches. This broken VCR is saving me a lot of money in video rentals.)

On another level, look at the absurdity of the situation. (How many times have I told that plumber. . . . ? I always thought a car meant liberty, mobility. . . .! With all my address books, I'm still missing some important telephone numbers. . . !) Imagine what a stand-up comic or a TV sit-com writer would do with the situation. Take it to the limits: a total flood in the house. . . . a Fellini-esque traffic jam. . . . losing contact with that friend forever. There is, fortunately, more comedy in our lives than tragedy: we're just less accustomed to seeing it and less adept at visualizing it.

Very often, other people can see the humor in our predicaments where we cannot, because they are not intimately and emotionally involved as we are. Don't take this as a sign of enmity or a lack of sympathy. They may very well empathize with our troubles, but their distinct separateness gives them an objective view that is quite different from our own subjective involvement. Thus, they may see facets of the situation that we can't see — including humor — and by stepping outside of ourselves and into their vantage point, we may get a valuable new perspective.

On still another plane, you might try a metaphysical approach. This may start out sounding funny, but be warned: it can lead to some serious insights. For example: That plumber has it in for me from a past life! This traffic jam is giving me a chance to breathe deeply and say my mantra. Perhaps, unconsciously, I really didn't want to call that person. Since the VCR is broken, I'll have time to catch up on my reading. That cancelled date is something I should have declined in the first place.

At first, these kinds of "rationalizations" may sound like just that: rationalizations. Or another form of *ad absurdum* humor. But over time, you will find they move from humor to a form of truth. It's not the same as viewing life as one long series of jokes — which it certainly isn't. But it is a way to lighten up, to make life more pleasant for ourselves and for others, and to enable us to focus seriously on those things that are truly serious. Only when we step back and see the bigger picture, or step around and see other pictures, or step in and see certain details, do we manage to get to the humor of the event, and sometimes, from that, to the truth. . . .which is the real punch line.

Notes

What makes me laugh?

_____

_____

_____

_____

What are my favorite jokes? Who are my favorite comedians?

_____

_____

_____

_____

What has happened this week that is really funny?

_____

_____

_____

_____

Other thoughts:

_____

_____

_____

_____

Chapter 5

OPTIMISM

To be seventy years young is sometimes far more cheerful and hopeful than to be forty years old.   /Oliver Wendell Holmes

If humor is an attitude toward present events, optimism is an attitude toward the future. Oddly enough, one can be very happy with the present, yet feel pessimistic about the future. Or conversely, be very unhappy in the present and feel optimistic about the future.

Why is this? I suggest that our view of the future is a reflection of our deepest learned reflexes, our childhood training and experiences. Were our parents positive thinkers? What did they tell us about the world? Were our simple needs and desires and expectations fulfilled? Or did we suffer distress and disappointment over and over again?

These early experiences turned us into optimists or pessimists, and whatever we experienced later in life, we kept the fundamental outlook: the glass was half full or half empty, we saw the doughnut or the hole. For example: Haven't you got a wonderful relationship? Yes, but it can't last. And a terrific job? Yes, but I won't be able to handle it. Or, on the other hand: Going through a bitter divorce? Yes, but I'll recover. And fired from your job? Yes, but I'll get a better one.

I'd guess that it's easier to turn an optimist into a pessimist than the other way around. It's easy to imagine how a lifetime of major disappointments, serious problems, successive setbacks, and unforeseen disasters could finally sour a person, if not actually lead to suicide. Fortunately, few of us have such a life of unremitting misery (though there are many who think they do).

On the other hand, don't we all know people who seem to have had every advantage in life, achieved every imaginable success in their private and public worlds, suffered no more than a stubbed toe or a bout of hayfever, and yet are always expressing their anxiety and complaining about their troubles. Clearly, they were raised on despair and dissatisfaction, and will never be content and optimistic.

How can we change our outlook from dark to bright? First of all, *can* we change it? I think so, but it takes tremendous determination.

The first step, as with everything, is awareness. Just being aware that you are continually unhappy, anxious or negative amounts to a tacit acknowledgement. Then, try making a list — a written list — of all the things you find wrong in your life, and a second list of what you think is going to go wrong in the future. If you're truly a confirmed pessimist, this list will be very long.

Next, make another list of everything that — you have to admit — is all right in your life. Things you can't honestly gripe about. Things other people actually envy or admire. Then, looking at your future list, write down item by item what the opposite would be. How many of those opposites are realistic, in the sense of being necessary and attainable? How many are grandiose pipedreams, inspired by ambitious parents, by your peer group, or by society's flavor-of-the-month celebrity? How many are petty pipedreams, unimportant and truly unnecessary to your well-being? Be honest: apart from good health and financial security, what things are critical, really crucial, to your existence? How much do you already have above and beyond this? How much could you actually do without?

Look at the low points of your life (we all have them, whether they're visible to others or not) and remember how you got through them. (If old hurts and defeats are still clinging to you, there's work to be done to abolish them.) No life is a perfect upward curve of advancement. There are jogs up and down.

The symbol for Yin and Yang is an even better image to describe how our lives flow: a process of constant change, with a small point of light in the dark part, and a small dark point in the light area. That point represents the ever-present potential, and while it is useful to remember the dark spot while we're traveling through a period of light, it's even more important to reflect on the speck of light while we're in the dark. That is not blind optimism: that is reality, and we must believe in it.

There's another side to optimism that has nothing to do with perceived reality — or reason; that in fact defies it. It is the invisible side of life where things are happening all the time. Sometimes our intuition can pick it up; usually it can't. It is the area where we find the unexpected, the *deus ex machina*, the miracle. (Whatever we can't explain by reason, we blithely label "a miracle".) It is what Deepak Chopra calls "the field of pure potentiality", where anything and everything can happen.

You don't have to be religious to believe in this realm. Simply affirm that things are happening far beyond our perception, deeper than our thoughts, out of our control yet subtly influenced by everything we do and think. Does it sound unscientific, unprovable? Physicists are working with these precepts every day, postulating the unknowable, naming the invisible: quarks, anti-quarks, gluons, mesons, positrons, neutrinos, black holes, strings. The Brothers Grimm could not have imagined such characters and such tales.

So why should it be difficult for us to believe in this realm, to believe that the cosmos is in a constant state of re-creation? And why should we not believe that all possibilities await us: we have only to develop the intelligence, the instinct, and the faith to attract and choose the right ones.

With this attitude and this certainty, it is impossible not

to be optimistic. The past is not an inescapable quagmire: it is the place we choose to stay in, or leave. Nor is the present a perplexing and persistent black hole: it is the clear result of our priorities and actions. Nor is the future a menacing cloud: it is where we will find all our new solutions, new ideas, new impetus.

This is optimism in its deepest, most meaningful sense. It is not a hop-scotch Polyanna game, it is not a race from reality. It *is* reality. . . . .but a reality that allows us to laugh and dream.

Notes

Am I *basically an optimist or a pessimist?*

_____

_____

_____

_____

What do I *feel optimistic about?*

_____

_____

_____

_____

What do I *feel pessimistic about?*

_____

_____

_____

_____

Other thoughts:

_____

_____

_____

_____

Chapter 6

TOLERANCE

No man can justly censure or condemn another, because indeed no man truly knows another. /Sir Thomas Browne

"Tolerance" sounds like a very unpleasant word. It raises visions of tight-lipped, hard-hearted people who "put up with" other people. While it rises far above hate, it seems to fall far short of love. Tolerance is not a visceral thing: it's rational.

Yet precisely for this reason, it should be an easily attainable goal. Hate can arise in a flash, from totally unconscious reactions, and it can last very, very long. Love, which takes time to germinate, is also unconsciously sourced, and it can vaporize in an instant. But tolerance is a conscious decision, a deliberately induced state of mind.

We can think about the noisy kids on the street, the restless tourists on our flight, the impolite salesperson, the inconsiderate driver, and fly into a rage. Or we can take out our worry beads, our incense, our mandala and our Bible, and try to calm ourselves into a state of transcendent love.

It doesn't work.

What does work is simply taking a deep breath and

stepping back, mentally. You think to yourself, "Is it worthwhile to let this get me upset?" You may go a step further and admit that kids are kids, that tourists on a crowded plane are always fidgety, that the salesperson may be ill, that the driver is having a rough day. But these excuses, though they may help, aren't really necessary. The important thing, the main thing, is that you stay in control of yourself, by simply allowing these things to be.

Certainly, where you can do something that might improve the situation, do it. Remind the listless waiter that you're still waiting for your dessert. Call the neighbors and politely ask them to turn down their radio. Return to the check-out counter and explain that you've been overcharged. But when those actions fail — and they often will — remember that we're living in a real world, not a perfect one, and that you are probably annoying, insulting or disappointing others almost as often as they are disturbing you!

Being tolerant in this way is not only doing a favor to others: it's doing a big favor to yourself. It's keeping your blood pressure down, it's saving your energy for more important activities, and it's setting an example that inevitably returns to you in kind. A smile is returned with a smile, a compliment with a compliment.

One's threshold of tolerance probably lowers naturally with age: "crochety old people" are almost a cliché, a caricature. But there are also crochety teenagers, crochety businessmen, crochety school teachers. If advancing age makes us more impatient and critical, it should also make us more leisurely and tolerant, for we have seen more, done more, learned more and endured more. We could almost be smug about that, but that would result in condescension, not tolerance.

Because it's a habit that can be acquired and practiced, like regular exercise, tolerance is not an impossible, pie-in-the-sky goal. By comparison, the admonition to "love your neighbor" is quite difficult. In fact, you would first have to define "love" in this particular context: romantic love?, filial love?, brotherly/sisterly love?, parental love?, altruistic, humanitarian, Platonic love? None of them seems appropriate — much less, attainable — especially while your neighbor's radio is blasting away. And we have, unfortunately, devalued and confounded the word "love" by applying it to so many things: "I love Ben and Jerry's ice cream", "I love to go shopping", "I love action movies". The Eskimos have more than a dozen words for snow; we need at least a dozen words for love.

So, getting back to tolerance: "Tolerate your neighbor" sounds both cruel and comical (the verb hits even harder than the noun), but "be tolerant of your neighbor" sounds all right. There is a sense of sharing and understanding, and that is probably the key to it all. We are sharing this life, this planet, with everyone else here at this time — even the homeless people on the other side of town and the maimed orphans in Kosovo and Sierra Leone. Our understanding of that is what makes tolerance possible, and beyond tolerance we may move to a higher level, which is not love, but compassion. To love everyone is not possible, and perhaps not even desirable, because "love" then would be diluted and diffused and passive, rather than strong and focused and active. But compassion for others is a limitless, timeless emotion that brings us closer to our own spirit. With compassion and understanding we can begin to right wrongs, help others, help the world.

Werner Erhard, the founder of est, used to say that "understanding is the booby prize". He was talking about the brain, not the heart. Cerebral activity for its own sake leads nowhere, accomplishes nothing. It is entertainment, or intellectual masturbation — pleasurable and self-satisfying, but not self-fulfilling. True understanding is not merely knowledge, it is wisdom, and wisdom emerges from an open heart and a tolerant mind.

Notes

In what ways am I tolerant?

_____

_____

_____

What can I absolutely not tolerate?

_____

_____

_____

Where in my life do I need to show more tolerance?

_____

_____

_____

Other thoughts:

_____

_____

_____

Chapter 7

HONESTY

Make yourself an honest man and then you may be sure there is one less rascal in the world. /Thomas Carlyle

We have all grown up with the youthful belief that "honesty is the best policy". George Washington and the cherry tree, "Honest Abe" Lincoln, even Pinocchio, have inculcated the idea that one must never lie. Or cheat. Or steal.

Naturally, as we grow older ("grow up"), we discover, and invent, exceptions to the rule. To save face, to save a friendship, to save a marriage, to save a job, we fabricate little fibs or outrageous whoppers and tell ourselves that, after all, the end justifies the means. Which it sometimes does. But we gradually learn that one lie or one misdeed always leads to another. A dishonest word or act is never sealed off completely from the rest of our lives: it creates fissures, requiring us to erect a scaffold of more lies to support it.

Even the seemingly more benign acts of omission create

imperceptible shock waves that eventually rock our lives. Breaking one's word, avoiding an obligation, evading an explanation, ignoring the rules of common courtesy, or blithely skipping out the door are cowardly escape routes. Sooner or later, the door we skipped out of is closed to us forever.

If we could see the effect of these actions, and non-actions, on our psyches — as the puppet could easily see on his nose — it would look like the eroded surface of the moon, or a sea of quicksand. Or a minefield, awaiting disaster. "I am a part of all that I have met", said the poet, hopefully with more satisfaction than misgiving. But we are also a part of all that we have said, all that we have done, and all that we have welched on. Our inner selves reflect our moral existence as surely as our outer selves reflect the food we ingest and the thoughts we hold.

This may be meaningless to you if you are someone who denies the existence of the psyche, or the soul, or the spirit (we can define these terms later), but you must admit that the human being is more than a one-dimensional physical entity: there are also the emotional and mental faculties, which are largely invisible and inscrutable. And they are not three separate, independent functions. Just try concentrating on a book or enjoying a meal when you're emotionally upset, or physically ill. Try helping a child with homework or planning a vacation when you're worried about your workload, or suffering a migraine. The state of each function — physical, mental and emotional — colors the other two, and when they are all out of balance, or functioning badly, the resulting hue, as any artist knows, is mud. (Not black, which is the absence of color entirely, and which quite accurately symbolizes death.)

Acknowledging this interconnectedness of our bodies, our minds, and our emotions can help us see how moments of love, of despair, of joy, of arrogance, of fear, of anxiety, of fatigue, of illness, of *everything* will surely affect the landscape of our existence. And the words we use and the actions we take (or avoid) are part of this: they are extensions or manifestations of our physical/mental/emotional state, for the better or the worse.

So a lie will have the same pernicious effect on us as a rotten piece of meat or a slap in the face. The difference is that we are doing it to ourselves. Therefore, we can prevent it. Deciding to live honestly is not only doing others a favor, but it is enhancing our own life. At this most fundamental and personal level, honesty is truly the best policy for our own well-being.

This does not mean we have to be "brutally" honest in all circumstances: pleasantly honest is fine. Honesty can even be cloaked in humor, dulling the sharp edge when it is necessary. And honesty should get easier as we get older, for we have less to simulate and less to hide. Young children are naturally honest because their egos haven't developed yet, and they haven't learned to weigh the stakes and see the consequences (things they learn eventually, of course, from the adult world). But that natural, spontaneous honesty often reappears in the elderly, who can be delightfully outspoken — when they are not cowed by doctors, nurses, and domineering family members; when they finally feel free enough and brave enough to let the chips fall where they may. This may sound like an echo of a line in Kris Kristofferson's song: "Freedom's just another word for nothing left to lose". The point is, there *is* nothing left to lose, except your integrity. And without that — without the nerve to state what you want, explain how you feel, do what you believe, and balance all that by following what is good — there can be no real health or happiness in one's life.

It takes only one step to get there: courage.

Notes

In what areas of my life have I been scrupulously honest?

_____

_____

_____

_____

Where and when in my life have I stretched or avoided the truth?

_____

_____

_____

_____

Where and when have I been dishonest to myself?

_____

_____

_____

_____

Other thoughts:

_____

_____

_____

Chapter 8

COURAGE

Courage is the thing. All goes if courage goes.
/Sir J. M. Barrie

We usually think of courage in terms of the young: daredevil kids in the playground, muscular athletes pushing themselves to the limit, men at war whose acts of bravery earn them medals. Courage in the elderly is often seen as stoic resignation (in the face of terminal illness or imminent death, for example). Courage in the elderly is seen as a last gasp, when there's nothing to do but hang on.

Why should this be so?

First of all, because we generally view courage as a physical manifestation, while it is truly much more than that. There is the courage of standing up for one's principles, the courage to speak one's mind, the courage to go against prevailing expectations and norms, the courage to experiment, innovate, renovate and discard. In short, the courage to be steadfastly oneself and, at the same time, the courage to change.

This is asking a lot of anyone, but especially of "older" people, who are notoriously fixed, rigid, set in their ways. In fact, for most of us, life is a long process of creating a basic pattern, or template, in our early years, repeating it over and over as time goes by, and settling into it comfortably and unquestioningly at twilight. There is nothing basically "wrong" with this if your primary goal is comfort and ease. It is a lot easier to put yourself on automatic pilot than to actually take the controls.

But that automatic pilot is an old, outmoded system of navigation. You're flying over the same old territory. And you're totally unprepared to handle unexpected turbulence. You might finally decide to turn the whole thing over to someone else — your spouse, your grown children, a trained caregiver — but then you might as well parachute out, because you no longer have control over anything: the speed, the altitude, or the destination.

This metaphor is not as far-fetched as it sounds. We all know people who, upon reaching retirement age, seem to drop out of the "real", active world entirely. (Although, admittedly, there are many who throw their energy into a substitute activity, such as golfing, fishing, or serving tyrannically on the board of a coop apartment building!) What has happened to the courage — the guts, the gumption, the gall — they had as company managers, trial lawyers, pediatric surgeons, creative directors, history professors? What has happened to their love of enterprise and discovery, their sense of their unique individuality? Why does a person leaving the world of work leave behind his identity and his spirit?

To some degree, the diminished sense of identity may be inevitable, for so much of our life is wrapped up in what we do, rather than who we are. We are more likely to be known and remembered as the CEO of General Whatever than as that warm, funny person who lived down the street. Fair enough. But we ourselves must also remember the active years of trials and triumphs and know that we are still the same person — on a different playing field, in a different game, but still capable of feats of courage.

In fact, because we have less at stake (materially and professionally), we can afford to be courageous and outrageous! If we were timid and self-effacing before, we can be outspoken and self-assertive now. This metamorphosis is often seen in today's women, particularly those who have gone through years of child-raising, house-keeping and husband-serving, and who — once the husband has retired or died or divorced them — suddenly make a startling shift in their lives. They go back to school for a degree, or get a part-time job, or start a small business, or take up a long-neglected hobby. That's courage. If the man is still around, he finds himself spending more time in the kitchen — which is a fine kind of role reversal. And maybe he really is glad to be out of the "rat race". But what a shame if he settles into complacency, and loses the passion and drive that marked his working years.

Much of this chapter has had to do with self-confidence and the courage to say "yes" — the courage to be active and positive and forthright. But there's another side to courage: the courage to say "no". And that has to do with self-respect and dignity.

Notes

When in my life have I shown real courage?

_____

_____

_____

_____

When in my life have I lacked courage, backed down, copped out?

_____

_____

_____

_____

What challenges are facing me now that require courage?

_____

_____

_____

_____

Other thoughts:

_____

_____

_____

_____

Chapter 9

DIGNITY

Being seventy is not a sin. /Golda Meir

Our contemporary world does not have much place for dignity. Apart from the pope or, on occasion, the pomp and circumstance surrounding a royal personnage, we see little evidence — and little appreciation — of dignified demeanor. Ever since the "Me Generation", we have been advised to flaunt our stuff, to let it all hang out, to spill our guts in public. We cry in front of strangers in mass consciousness-raising groups, and we expose our most private lives in front of television cameras. We applaud the exhibitionist pop stars and movie stars, emulate the loud talk-show hosts, and gobble up the tabloid scandals. Every life is potentially an open book; nothing is too sacred to be left untouched.

Is this a sign of absolute democracy? The final abolition of class distinction, making everyone "equal"? Does democracy really demand full and complete disclosure, and the inevitable descent to the lowest common denominator?

Will the invasion of privacy bring about an end to

hypocrisy, or will it engender a new form of hypocrisy that says, in effect, "I admitted it, therefore I'm absolved". There's a big difference between what Jean-Paul Sartre called "transparency" and what the media calls "exposure". It's like the difference between a photograph and an X-ray.

This new phenomenon, our collective X-ray vision, automatically implies that we are looking for trouble — for a fracture, for a rupture, for some anomaly. And of course, we find it — either through the process of "investigative reporting" or with the complicity and connivance of the publicity-seeker himself. The next step is public surgery, followed by public convalescence, followed by resurrection or death. This is how the cult of personality has usurped the creed of character. Or, how "characters" have replaced "character".

It has been a long time since we stood in awe of a president, or of any authority figure. Are we reacting negatively to authority *per se*, or to the person who wields it? It has also been a long time since bank clerks and salespersons dropped "Mr." and "Mrs." and began calling us by our first names. Are they pretending to be friendly, and why? Are we pretending to enjoy it?

These are very diverse questions, and they raise many issues. But at the core of them all is the fact that respect, reserve, privacy and dignity are fast disappearing from our world. We speak often enough of "human dignity", but this is so abstract that it means very little, and can therefore be applied to any contradictory propositions. For example, is it a sign of "human dignity" to insist on saving an embryo, or to consider first the well-being of the woman carrying it? Is it more respectful of "human dignity" to prolong the life of a dying patient by all the artificial means available, or to allow that person to expire peacefully? Is it expressing "human dignity" to keep a severely disabled child in a regular classroom, or rather to place that child in a special care facility?

Fortunately, in our own lives, we have only to answer for ourselves, not make rules for everybody. So we can determine where our boundaries are. As examples: we do not have to answer all personal questions; we do not have to accept rudeness from a headwaiter (or anyone); we do not have to cave in to requests for help or money; we do not have to be paragons of patience when a dental appointment is running an hour late.

Dignity is based on self-respect, and if we don't acquire that when we're young (which is understandable, because we still don't know quite who we are), then the perfect time to develop it is as we're growing older. As years go by, we learn what is important to us and what isn't, what makes sense and what doesn't, and where exactly we draw the line. We have a better sense of our own worth, and in a sense, we *are* worth more. The knowledge and experience one acquires throughout life are unimaginable to us in our early years. We can take pride in it — even in the failures and mistakes

— because it is unique and unreplicable.

Pride and self-respect and dignity seem to be attributes that appear only as we age, and this is as it should be. Who ever heard of a dignified adolescent or child? Dignity gives rise to the *"grande dame"* and the elder statesman. It reinforces the foundation of our lives, and strengthens our character. It keeps us from flitting, fluttering and fumbling; from squandering our energy and splintering our time; from playing a simpering victim or being truly victimized.

Even a beggar can beg with dignity. Dignity is an affirmation of our self, and it is a self that we must learn to value as we grow up and grow older.

When in my life have I been shown the most respect?

In what situations do I sense a lack of respect? How do I react?

What bolsters my sense of dignity?

Other thoughts:

Chapter 10

FAITH

Life without faith is an arid business. /Sir Noël Coward

We know that a lifetime — any lifetime — will be full of joys and sadness. There will be periods of monotony and despair and challenge and crisis. One life is never like any other, so it often is difficult for us to understand and comfort another person whose experience and scope and timing are so different from ours. In fact, we usually have quite enough difficulty framing our own situation and understanding what our own life is about.

And yet, we can perceive the parallels, the parameters, of our lives and others'. There are common denominators to all human experience, which we see in myths, in literature, in theater. Our personal experience is both unique and universal.

The question is: how do we move from the unique to the universal? And why should we?

We should do it because in limiting our perspective to just our own lives we miss a great deal of knowledge and enrichment. Discovering commonality with others — either through friends and acquaintances or through books and plays — opens our mind and our heart. We realize, at a most basic level, that we are not alone. Our egocentric stance — our anguish, our pride, our fear — is ever so slightly tipped, and we move a bit outside ourselves, to a broader realm.

As to how we do this: psychoanalysis or other therapies can help; so can the study of philosophy and spiritual paths; and for some, the answer is religion. But simply talking to others, sharing our experiences and ideas in an open, non-judgmental way, will gradually help us see the truth: that each of us is on a journey. Our points of departure differ, our routes may cross and converge and separate, and our destinations are unknown. But that is the wonder and the mystery of it.

This is the knowledge that should bring us to a final leap of faith. Not so much a leap, at this point, as a natural progression. We have all heard the dictum that it is not the goal but the journey that counts. Or, as the old French Line used to advertise: "Getting there is half the fun". Sometimes it may not look like much fun, but who ever heard of a lifelong voyage without some rough seas and stormy weather?

To close our eyes to this truth — the necessity and the inevitability of our journey — is to stunt our lives and to shrink our dreams. We will be locked in a prison of despair, with dashed hopes and unrealized potential. Understanding that each of us was born to make this journey, this personal odyssey can be seen as a source of discovery and growth, not as a perilous obstacle course or a frustrating test of endurance. Endurance is required, naturally, but in a spirit of openness and gladness, and with the certainty — the faith — that all is going as it should.

For indeed it is.

Faith involves looking at the present and the future, but we must also look at the past in a spirit of reconciliation and release. It is all too easy to recall our mistakes, our disappointments, our failures, our pain, and brood over them year after year. This is like watering a garden that is overgrown with weeds: inevitably, the weeds take over. Even prolonged psychoanalysis can have that effect, for by continually rehashing and reiterating our woes, we are renewing and retaining and reinforcing them.

It takes not simply faith but determination to say "enough is enough". Just as in a destructive relationship or a dead-end job we must finally move out, and on, so must we let go of our past. Blaming our parents, our lovers, our colleagues is totally unproductive. We must understand that they did the best they could do — unsatisfactory as it may have been — and while we may not reach a point of full forgiveness, we can certainly achieve a state of quiet resignation, and acceptance.

Besides that, we have to acknowledge that we ourselves

were part of the problem: whatever the reasons, we stuck with the job, we remained in the relationship, and karmic philosophy would even say we chose our parents. What have we learned from it? That is the question we should be asking, rather than laying blame, seeking revenge, flagellating ourselves, or giving up. And do we now have the wisdom and the will to avoid, or better handle, similar situations in the future? That is where faith finally comes in: when we recognize that we have survived unhappiness, have learnt some lessons from it, and need not go through the same difficulties again.

Of course, there will be other challenges, other obstacles, other problems. But understanding and insight into our past trials — and sincere reconciliation — will give us the self-confidence to confront future ones. Self-confidence gives us faith in ourselves; faith in the life process gives us peace.

Peace, after all, is where our paths should be leading. After the turbulence of youth, and the uncertainties of adulthood, our later years should be a time of peacefulness: peace with ourselves, with others, and with life.

Notes

What do I deeply believe in?

Where do these beliefs come from?

When is my faith shaken? What restores it?

Other thoughts:

PART II

Chapter 11

THE MIND

Age is strictly a case of mind over matter. If you don't mind, it doesn't matter. /Jack Benny

Simplicity, curiosity, humor, optimism, tolerance, honesty, courage, dignity and faith: these are attributes that balance and enhance our lives at any age. The first four are pertinent to our "exterior" existence: our dealings with the world around us. The last group of four have to do with our "interior" world: our principles and our self-image. Tolerance, in the middle, is like the link between them: being tolerant obviously relates to something outside ourselves, but it is a response that comes from within.

The disconnection, or disparity, between one's outer life and inner life is one of the main causes of unhappiness. A successful life in the material world means little if one is emotionally insecure or spiritually bankrupt. And the emotional or spiritual side will be frustrated if it cannot be expressed or manifested in the physical world. We know at a gut level when some aspect of ourselves is being thwarted or denied, and we also know — or sense — when one part of us is acting out of sync with the others. We know it because our relationships falter, our work gets frantic or flat, our nerves jangle, and our health deteriorates.

Simply seeing ourselves in this tripartite way — physical, emotional and spiritual — is a good way to begin to integrate all three aspects. By mentally visualizing your material goals, your emotional needs, and your moral values (or ethical principles), you may figure out if any one area is in conflict with another. Write it out like a spreadsheet, across three columns. It's a good way to see it concretely in black and white.

For example, do you need the security of a good job, or a close relationship, or a comfortable home, yet at the same time crave excitement, freedom and travel? Is it more important to you to have a successful career, or an active social life, or a close-knit family? Do you worry most about your finances, or your marriage, or your future? Usually, the things that bothered us as young people are the things that continue to bother us as we grow older. Patterns persist, and grow more ingrained. So as the years pass, we may have more pain from the unsolved problems, but we also have a larger view, a deeper perspective, of them. This in turn can help us decide that the time has come when we must deliberately change course. And often, this also means bravely letting go.

This is hard to do after years of habit, but at the same time it's easier, for we can see clearly how the old ways haven't worked. Therefore, mentally, change will make sense. Our mind can then play with ideas, visualize them, choose one approach that we think is best, and begin to impress it on our consciousness. It is a form of creative thinking, and positive thinking, that eventually ignites the will. "A thought once thought can never be unthought", and by dwelling on the new, positive concept we can gradually move toward action.

Emotion can help or hinder the process. Fear, anxiety and guilt can hold us back from positive change, because they are internalized; they paralyze us, and contract our field of action. But anger, despair and frustration can actually hasten change, for they are emotions that seek to be externalized and expressed. Recognizing these feelings and relating them to our new concepts, our new thought patterns, gives tremendous power to the process of change.

Emotion, after all, informs the mind, and mind and emotion together define the soul. By deadening our feelings or denying them, we are dulling our mental powers. And conversely, when we fail to use our minds productively and creatively, we are shrinking our emotional capacity. One is linked to the other.

Innumerable books have been written on ways to change thought patterns and, subsequently, behavior. Creative visualization is one effective way. Imagining, and even writing down, over and over again, how you would like your life to be — rather than dwelling on the mess you perceive — can actually change the brain's frame of reference.

Meditation is another technique. Alone, it can quiet the mind, by avoiding distracting thoughts and thereby distancing us from them. Meditation plus auto-suggestion is enormously powerful. It literally brain-washes our mind of old grimey thought patterns and replaces them with new "clean" ones. (A qualified hypnotherapist can help with this.)

Rebirthing, psychoanalysis, and various forms of group therapy are other techniques, but for most of us, who live in the twilight zone of dissatisfaction, and not in the midnight zone of dark desperation, intensive measures are not always necessary. Sometimes a trusted friend, an intelligent mentor, or a sympathetic counsellor can help us discuss the problems, bring some objective insights, and stay in touch with us as we go through our process. This "monitoring" is essential: it is all too easy to give up, or to slip back unconsciously into old thinking habits and old behavior patterns. Having a written record, and an advisor to back us up, helps to keep us on track.

Above all, it's important not to trick oneself into thinking that change and transformation are impossible or unnecessary. Chronic dissatisfaction and chronic unhappiness are states of mind that have more to do with our inner attitudes than our outer environment. We can decide whether our bottle of wine is actually half full or half empty; whether a weekend in the country will be restful or boring; whether a course of study is going to be stimulating or arduous; whether a new friendship is going to be enriching or depleting. In each case, our attitude and expectations will define and determine the outcome.

It is hard for most of us, raised in a world based on empirical science and hard-nosed facts, to accept this premise. Yet more and more, we are living in a "virtual" world, where the boundaries between "real" and "unreal" are blurred. Dan Rather and David Letterman are more frequent visitors in our home than the next-door neighbor. Watching a film, we are transported to places we will never visit, and we get involved in dramas that will never occur in our lives. We have more information at our fingertips in one issue of The New York Times than the average person acquired in a lifetime one hundred years ago, but it is second-hand information that has been gathered and diffused by other people, not by us. In a way, our active *participation* in life is narrowing down to mere *perception* of life. We are relying more and more on our mental (i.e., virtual) activity to sustain us in the physical realm.

But while we are less active physically, we must recognize that our "passive" process of perception has a real impact on external objects and events. This was proven by physicists many decades ago, who demonstrated that by simply observing a moving particle, we alter the particle's course. In the same way, when we observe something in our life, or focus our attention on it, we are projecting energy into it that will alter it in some way. The object of our attention can be a person, a problem, or an idea; the crucial element is what *kind* of attention or energy we are directing at it — negative or positive — for the object will respond in kind.

Most people today, at the dawn of the third millennium, will insist this is impossible. But the concept is not just a new-fangled proposition from theoretical physics; it is much older than that. It goes back to very ancient traditions and religions that acknowledged the power of mind over matter, and its most basic expression is the belief in the power of prayer.

The agnostic and the atheist may recoil at this statement, but that is because we commonly define prayer as calling upon God for help. But God, or our concept of Him/Her, is not in the picture at all. Prayer, in its truest sense, is communication with ourself — or with our inner Self. It is plumbing the depths of our most profound desires and fears. It is focusing attention on an aspect of our life that requires attention. . . . and probably, correction.

Prayer can also be a form of thanksgiving: it is an affirmation of appreciation, and it reinforces whatever in our life is going well.

Seen in this light, prayer is more closely aligned with psychology than with religion. Religion, in fact, can hinder the process, for it interjects dogma and ritual and figureheads that block our direct access to our Selves. Why take a circuitous route, full of detours and distractions, when we can make the journey simply and surely on our own?

What does all this have to do with growing older?

It has to do with the mind, which does not age as quickly or as irreversibly as we once believed. Brain cells — and especially, neural connections between the cells — continue to function and reproduce throughout our life, researchers now confirm. So just as we must care for our bodies, with exercise and good nutrition, we must care for our brains, with mental exercises and stimulation. Reading books and a daily newspaper, doing crossword puzzles and quizzes and games, enrolling in a course and attending lectures — these are some of the things that keep our minds alert and active.

It's become a truism that we use less than ten percent of our brainpower. Imagine what merely doubling that, to twenty percent, could do! Properly cared for and vigorously used, the brain could actually assume many functions that we now delegate to other people, or that we simply dismiss. Applying our minds to visualization, meditation and prayer, we could overcome illness, acquire more energy, enhance our relationships, and discover new sources of enrichment in our lives. And that's only the beginning. It is not too far-fetched to imagine the day when the human race will be able to communicate through mental telepathy, travel through virtual time zones, and transmute base metals into gold.

Chapter 12

THE BODY

I haven't asked you to make me young again. All I want is to go on getting older. /Konrad Adenauer (to his doctor)

Usually, when people talk or write about aging, the emphasis is on the physical aspect: the diseases, the deterioration, the disabilities, and the myriad disorders. Because the physical aspect is so visible, it naturally dominates our view of aging.

So why hasn't it been discussed here, up until now?

Because, precisely, it *is* such a dominant theme and because so much attention is already being paid to it. We can pick up innumerable books on cardiology, cancer, arthritis, osteoporosis, nutrition, exercise, and other medical subjects and learn a great deal from them. We can consult with our physicians, undergo exhaustive examinations, and follow the latest fads on the market. Sometimes we will find real relief to real problems. Sometimes not. Sometimes, we have to understand that the "problems" themselves are actually symptoms: there may be underlying reasons why a heart is weak, why bones are brittle, why one is obese, and these reasons are very likely to originate in the mind.

This is not to say they are imaginary; most sick people are definitely not hypochondriacs. But what we think affects what we feel, and our language reflects this poignantly: I'm heartbroken, heartsick, a bundle of nerves, sick to my stomach, fed up, sick and tired, eating my heart out, I can't stomach it, get off my back, you've got a chip on your shoulder. . . .

Louise Hay has written extensively on physical symptoms and how they relate to mental and emotional states. Deepak Chopra has done perhaps more than anyone to illustrate and confirm the mind-body connection, an idea that western medicine has rejected for far too long. And now, as we learn more about the human immune system and neuro-receptors, we are beginning to realize that illness is not merely a question of the body being invaded by viruses and bacteria, for we have millions of "germs" living inside us all the time. Why do we succumb, and to what do we succumb, at some given time? Fundamentally, it is a question of our own defense system, which in turn is a function of our knowledge, our attitudes, our emotions, and our beliefs.

The day will surely come, very soon in this new century, when we will look back at twentieth century medicine with horror and disbelief, much as we look back at leeches and blood-letting today. Anaesthetizing the entire organism with chemicals, cutting and gouging into living flesh, replacing malfunctioning organs with foreign bodies, zapping damaged cells and tissue with deadly X-rays — these are brutal measures that will one day be replaced by gentler, wiser practices. We will learn how to work with receptors and transmitters and blockers, how to heal at a hormonal and genetic level, how to create new compatible organs with stem cells, and most of all, how to use the powers of the mind to prevent and cure illness, to heal and regenerate organs and limbs, and to achieve that ancient ideal: *mens sana in corpore sano*. Or maybe we'll turn it around, and strive for a sound body in a sound mind!

For the mind is essential. All too often, we see cases where "life" is sustained artificially, where life functions are performed by machines, and we admit the patient has become a "vegetable". What we fail to recognize, however, is that the body and mind have, at that point, split apart: one is no longer attached to the other. The mind no longer controls the body, and is not receptive to the body, and the disease becomes "terminal". Interestingly, medical practitioners do recognize the primacy of the brain, in spite of themselves, for they say death has finally occurred when someone is "brain dead". But they are still confused in cases of coma: is the person alive or dead?

Alzheimer's disease is another confusing issue. We still don't know what causes the cumulative and irreversible dysfunction of the brain, nor why this "new" disease has arisen. We may link it to contemporary lifestyles (fast, frustrating and stressful); to chemicals and pollutants in our food, water and air; even to the fact that we are living longer, having conquered such old diseases as tuberculosis and malaria and smallpox and polio; and that therefore, inevitably, new diseases will arise as we age.

This last hypothesis may come closest to the truth, but with a twist. We have indeed "conquered" many diseases of the body, because ever since the Renaissance our bodies have been of paramount importance to us. (The body has even been called "the seat of the soul", though more correctly it's the reflection, or material manifestation, of the soul.) But perhaps we are getting to the point in our evolution where, having overcome many bodily (physical) problems, we are being directed to turn our attention to the mental (psychological) realm, which is a higher plane of existence and a more powerful one.

This is to suggest that Alzheimer's may be a disease of our age, a disease whose time has come. For in such diseases as tuberculosis, malaria, smallpox and polio, there is a direct physical connection, clear evidence of cause and effect: unsanitary conditions, a mosquito's bite, a bacterial or viral infection. Cancer is not so simple: it is forcing us to recognize and acknowledge the relationship between mind and body. Where, for example, do cancer cells arise? In the ovaries or the breast? In the prostate or the colon? In the bones or the brain? That is likely to indicate the place — metaphorically — where the patient is feeling the most stress in his/her life. Even lung cancer, which we relate directly to an external source — tobacco — raises the question: Why is this particular person a heavy smoker to begin with? Why is he drugging himself with nicotine?

And even as we struggle with cancer, Alzheimer's has arisen as a wholly new mystery, seemingly centered on the brain and the brain's functions.

The fact is, our whole paradigm of disease is changing, and we must look for new answers and new solutions. Rather than running off to consult with the appropriate specialist when a problem arises, perhaps we should seek out a "generalist" — someone who can observe and understand the mind-body connection, and work with the whole person to reestablish balance and well-being.

And even before we get to that point, we ourselves must take care of ourselves. This does not mean simply gorging on vitamins, sweating out at the gym every day, or becoming paranoid about what we eat. (Julia Child has said, "If you're afraid of what you eat, of course it will harm you".) It means maintaining a certain degree of moderation and regularity in your life: eating patterns, sleeping patterns, relaxation patterns. This is not as boring as it sounds. It is simply giving yourself the solid structure from which you can improvise and deviate from time to time, without real danger. It is the loom, the warp and the woof, on which you can weave some new patterns without fear of the whole thing unravelling.

There are small ways, too, in which we can enhance our lives and our well-being. The way we walk, or stand, or sit in a chair reveals not only how we feel but how we feel about ourselves. While youth is depicted, literally and figuratively, as growing up, age seems to be a process of growing down. We slump, we shuffle, we sink into our armchairs and struggle to get out. The image we have of ourselves is clearly reflected in the way we use our bodies: it is our body language. When you see yourself as old, decrepit, debilitated, you will move that way. When you see yourself as youthful, healthy and active — and happy — your body will respond.

Moreover — and this is still surprising to many people — consciously using your body in a positive way will affect your mental outlook, for just as there is a psycho-somatic (mind to body) link, there is also a somato-psychic (body to mind) link. This is the basis of yoga: practicing certain exercises and assuming certain positions will eventually bring a sense of peace and calm to the mind. And in daily life, walking upright and briskly, standing straight and tall, sitting erect and poised, will not only project an image of youthfulness to others, but to yourself as well!

And what about artificial help?: cosmetic surgery, liposuction, hair transplants? Surely, these are being used and abused by many people today as quick fixes that merely camouflage their aging process, rather than enhance it. Sculpting a young face on an old body is rather grotesque.

Carving a young body on an old mind ("old" as opposed to "mature") is equally bizarre. Yet there seems to be some valid justification for a certain degree of "improvement": if it truly makes us feel better about ourselves, if it corrects a long-standing blight on our self-image, if it helps us project the way we truly feel and the age we feel. A sixty-year old who wants to look twenty is clearly out of touch with him/herself and out of sync with life in general. A sixty-year old entertainer who needs to keep up appearances (and keep on working) may have a better criterion. (Though of course we may question why our society demands age-proof entertainers.) A sixty-year old who is active, youthful in mind and spirit, and happy in life may simply decide that the outer person does not truly reflect the inner person, and removing a few years surgically may bring it all into a better balance.

So harmony is the key. In dress, too, we must decide what not only reflects us best, but what expresses us most accurately. Growing older does not mean growing somber. It means understanding our bodies, our way of life, and our personal preferences. It means dressing comfortably and appropriately (for ourselves, for the occasion) and leaving some room for fun and fantasy, be it a feather boa, a wild tie, or an extravagant piece of jewelry. If you were a gray-flannel-suit person at thirty, there's no reason why you can't be a flower child at seventy. Only beware of looking like a clone (and a clown) of your teenage grandchildren! Individuality and even eccentricity are positive values; desperate and blind imitation are utterly foolish.

At any age, our bodies are important — as mechanisms that sustain our life, as sources of pleasure, and as symbols of who and what we are. We must resist the temptation to turn over our bodies unquestioningly to the hordes of "experts" who claim to know what is best for us. Getting in touch with ourselves, believing in ourselves, and, if need be, doing our own investigation, will help us much more.

The body is not to be reviled or revered: it is to be respected and enjoyed.

Chapter 13

THE EMOTIONS

I feel a feeling which I feel you all feel. /Bishop George Ridding (a sermon in 1885)

If the body is still a field of exploration, and the mind is still an unsolved puzzle, then the emotions are an unfathomable enigma.

Anger, love, fear, joy, grief, guilt, desire, hate — where do they come from? From the subconscious, we say, but what is that? Or from chemical and hormonal reactions, but what triggers them? Or from our upbringing, or genetics, or from past life experiences. Our theories are as varied and as elusive as the emotions they try to comprehend.

Perhaps this is only just; perhaps there has to be a part of the human being that is incomprehensible, that approaches the realm of mystery and spirit. For in a sense, the emotions *are* a manifestation of spirit. They defy empirical analysis, they follow no laws, they are immutably fixed or wildly erratic, they interrelate with the body and mind but in ways that are difficult to perceive and almost impossible to control. That is why we resort to tranquilizers and amphetamines and alcohol and psychoanalysts — anything that will ease the ache or calm the chaos.

Chaos, in fact, is an apt description of the life of the emotions as we see it. If, traditionally, we have viewed the body in a mechanistic way, and the mind, recently, as a relativistic process, then it's natural that the emotions appear chaotic. This parallels the evolution of scientific thinking, which has evolved from a mechanistic view of the universe to a relativistic view to a point where we must recognize that chaos — or indeterminacy — also exists. This is the subatomic realm where cause and effect are not operating; nor is relativity. And this is what often seems to be true of the emotions, as we try to understand and control them.

Why do we sometimes feel love and hate toward the same object? (The so-called love-hate relationship.) Why do we anticipate an event with both excitement and apprehension? Why do we recall something with both joy and regret? Why are we sometimes so confused about a situation that we cannot "sort out our feelings"? Why are we sometimes stymied or stumped — or catapulted into action — by a barrage of contradictory and incomprehensible emotions?

Of course, there are degrees of emotionality. Some people have a smaller, stricter range of feelings or are less influenced by them: the "cerebral" types. And there are others — the "feeling" types — who are highly susceptible to their emotions. Yet all of us have this emotional matrix, just as we have a body and a mind, that influences and colors nearly every aspect of our lives. And still we do not understand it.

Before understanding, there is awareness, which is a form of acknowledgement. Our emotions must be brought to light and honored; we all know the havoc wreaked by repressed emotions and denial. This very act of awareness creates a space, a gap, a pause. In that pause, we can ask ourselves what we are actually feeling, why we are feeling it, and whether that feeling is appropriate to the situation. This is the work of our mind, which is best equipped to assess and evaluate both the situation and our feelings. But the next question is equally important: In feeling this, am I hurting myself or helping myself? In other words, is this emotion going to help me resolve or improve the situation, or assist me in some way?

This may sound idiotic, but remember that emotions are simply the fuel that powers our will, which in turn is harnessed by our mind. The emotions, the will, and the mind are like the fuel, the engine, and the driver: any one of them, alone, goes nowhere; two of them alone are also ineffective; only with all three operating together can there be effective activity, meaningful movement, and harmony in one's life.

For the mind (the driver) is impotent and passive. (In fact, "an active mind" is a bit of an oxymoron, because minds don't act!) And the will, like any engine, can wear out and rust with disuse. (And self-destruct with *mis*use.) The emotions, in themselves, are powerful fuel (high octane!), and volatile, but they are neither bad nor good. Fear, for example, can save us from danger or it can hold us back from an enriching experience. Guilt can lead us to make proper amends or it can keep us locked in a prison of self-recrimination. Anger can expose and clarify an ambiguous situation, or it can kill. Even love, which we always think of as a positive emotion, can be destructive, when it turns to smothering possessiveness or obsession, or when it's focused on an inappropriate object.

This is not to suggest that we can, or should, always analyze and edit our emotions, any more than we should ignore them. As stated earlier, they often arise from obscure sources and act like free radicals, in weird and unpredictable ways. We must honor that as a given, just as we would never say to a grieving friend, "You shouldn't be so unhappy. Snap out of it." That is denigrating the friend and discrediting her feelings. We should not do this to ourselves either. But we can and should try to comprehend why certain emotions have appeared in a given situation, and whether they will help or hinder us there. Then, if we can't alter the emotional impediment, at least we can act in ways — rational ways — that will soften it or circumvent it entirely. (For example, "I'm furious about this, but I'd better broach it gently or I'll ruin our vacation.") This is how mind and emotions can work together.

Much of our confusion about emotions is due to traditional religious precepts, which are very contradictory in this area — as in many others. The entire range of emotional expression — what is permitted and what is not — can be found in religion, from puritanical repression to saintly ecstasy (both, indeed, under the cloak of Christianity), from impassioned Hasidic scholarship to whirling dervish trances, from Buddhist serenity to Hindu frenzy. Is it any wonder we are confused?

In our own lives and in our families, we are taught, directly or indirectly, how we should react to certain things. This is a path leading surely and sadly to rigid patterns of behavior. Just as bad, we may never have any kind of emotional education or encouragement, and we grow up in total turmoil (overreacting) or borderline autism (underreacting).

Reacting, in fact, is the key concept here, and the key problem. Many of our emotions, though coming from "inside", are triggered by external events. Or, unconsciously, we set up the events, such as a confrontation with a spouse, an argument with a child, an impossibly overcharged schedule at the office, a dinner party with people we "owe" but don't really like. Naturally, we react explosively or sullenly, storm out the door or pop a Valium, and simply reinforce the destructive emotional pattern.

What we need to understand is to what degree we are falling into these traps or setting them up ourselves, and recognize that we are then reacting like mindless robots. Unfortunately, most of us live our lives in this reactive mode, rather than being *proactive*. Proactive means taking the time to reflect, to figure out what we want, devising a way to achieve it, and then taking the steps. It is a *response* to something, not a reaction. And therein lies the difference — the difference between a thoughtful appraisal and a knee-jerk reflex.

Knee-jerk reflexes are especially common when we're exposed to the emotions of another person. Then, it takes all our patience and wisdom to stay calm and try to maintain some balance — in ourselves and in the situation. A friend who is sobbing, a child who is screaming, a parent who is carping, a co-worker who is sulking — we have to learn how to handle these outbursts with compassion and intelligence, and not get sucked into the storm. The ultimate response — and sometimes the best — is just to walk away, and let it blow over.

But of course, many emotional states are positive, pleasant, and just as contagious as the negative ones. They can be brought on by music, by a good meal, by a party, by a walk in the woods, by meditation, by almost anything that is innately life-enhancing. These are the emotions we want to cultivate and share; these are the emotions that move our lives forward. A word of caution here, however: what you feel must be real — real pleasure, real relaxation, real appreciation as you participate in the activity, which means getting into it fully and openly. You can't fake happiness or love or contentment, not for very long, and the phony feeling eventually will boomerang.

Positive thinking, which certainly has its merits, must never be carried to the point where it becomes a mask or a camouflage. This is so often the case today in America, where the smiling face, the "have-a-nice-day", the "I'm-OK-you're-OK" attitude may actually be blanketing an acre of woes. It is a form of avoidance, or even denial, which keeps others at a distance and prevents the sufferer from coming to terms with his suffering.

Psychologists are starting to examine this "tyranny of the positive attitude", and they are concluding that a little angst is a good thing. It is like a reality check, or a private game of truth or consequences. Being aware of one's unhappiness or anxiety, and expressing it, can help us come to terms with it, resolve it, or integrate it positively into our lives. Or simply live with it, as we may have to live with flat feet or a receding hairline.

Perfection, after all, is an unattainable ideal; why not settle for excellence? Instead of a perfect relationship with one's in-laws, how about a good relationship? Instead of a perfect job, how about an interesting one? Instead of raising perfect children, how about raising decent, happy human beings?

When things go wrong, as they do, we have every right to complain and kick and cry. It would be unnatural not to. The point is not to wallow in it, nor, at the other extreme, bandage it over with artificial cheer. Neither response is a solution. But acknowledging the negative feelings, expressing them, understanding them, and gradually letting them go to make room for more positive ones, is the way we can best help that part of ourselves that we call our spirit.

Chapter 14

THE SOUL

What is a man profited, if he shall gain the whole world, and lose his own soul? /The Bible (Matthew, 16:26)

A discussion of the soul could be material for an entire book: why even try to bring it in here?

Because it is an aspect of our life that gets more pronounced, more prominent, as the years go by. We rarely speak of a child's soul, but as we grow older and those around us grow older — and especially, as we go through trials and triumphs and eventually face death (including the deaths of those close to us) — we begin to see another dimension, and we call it the soul.

This is not necessarily a religious vision, though all religions speak of it. It is, rather, an invisible synthesis of all that we were from the beginning (from before birth), plus all that we have become. It is the original raw material, to which has been added our specific life experience. It is unique, and it is immortal.

The immortality of the soul is due to its return, again

and again, in the process we call reincarnation. This is a concept that is difficult for most westerners to accept. Raised on a theology of heaven and hell, life and afterlife, we find it hard to imagine serial existences. This life, we believe, is here and now; it's the only one; we have only one shot at it; when it's over it's over.

This is a dreary and desperate view of things. That is not to say that one ought to believe in reincarnation because it is more consoling (which it is). But it is actually more scientific. We know that nothing is ever lost in the universe: matter reverts to energy and energy re-manifests as matter. So when a physical body "dies", as we say, its energy is released. That clump of energy is the soul. We can only guess where it goes, and for how long. But it is certain to become manifest again, in the eternal cycle of existence.

If we accept that there is, or may be, a soul, we can rightfully ask "Why?". What is its purpose, its function, its significance? And if we understand that, how do we nourish it, care for it, integrate it into our lives?

Starting from our definition of the soul — as a synthesis of all that we were and all that we are becoming — we must conclude that the soul encompasses everything: body, mind and spirit; action, thought and emotion. It is both the blueprint of our birth and the ledger of our growth. Whatever we do in this life becomes an indelible part of it — a permanent part of its energy pattern.

This may seem terribly abstract and abstruse, but think

of the ways in which we speak of the soul: selling one's soul, with all my soul, heart and soul, body and soul, save your soul, he has no soul, seeking one's soulmate, a lost soul, an old soul. All these expressions are speaking of something very concrete, something that not only includes body, mind and spirit, and interacts with them, but also exists apart from them.

In its apartness, the soul seems to be on a different, higher plane. It speaks to us in dreams; it gives us flashes of *déjà vu*; it soothes us when its needs are being met; and it discomforts us when we ignore it, contradict it, or sell it short. It is, in a way, our conscience, and a reflection of our character, but even more, because it has survived and evolved over so many lifetimes, it is a storehouse of our personal truth and wisdom, however great or small.

When we do something that is clearly illegal or immoral, we have a legal system that steps in and administers retribution or punishment (hopefully). But when we do something that runs counter to our soul, we suffer a worse punishment: a gradual gnawing away of our very essence, a diminution of our self-respect and a loss of our credibility.

This sounds very harsh, but the soul is a powerful entity. It is the closest connection we have to God, or to godliness. When one says — as is often said today — "the answer is within you", we are saying that the soul knows. The body, the mind and the emotions may give us hints and signals, but these signals are coming first from the soul.

So the soul's function is partly to be a watchdog — to keep us on track — and to further our development and growth. It can also help keep us from repeating mistakes — mistakes from past lives or from the present life. It can remind us of higher truths and loftier ideals than those we practice now. It can reward us with peace.

Peace with others and peace with ourselves cannot be had while our soul is in turmoil. And turmoil arises when the soul is offended. Sometimes, crafty substitutions and creative solutions will work — any experienced cook will tell you that! But a mean little compromise, a nasty omission, or a gross digression will weaken the integrity of the soul, and set it back not only for this lifetime but for other lifetimes to come.

The soul is what holds us together, and it holds on. Our bodies may be broken, our minds confused, our emotions tangled, but the soul — even when it is ignored and betrayed and trampled — stays with us. It may be severely damaged and corrupted, it may even appear to be "lost", but it's retrievable. The admonition to "save your soul" means simply coming back to your origins, to the essence of yourself — which is your soul — and caring for it.

How is this done? People who have had out-of-body experiences or near-death encounters seem to have learned. Their life focus shifts from the narrow to the broad, from the specific to the general. At the same time, there is a shift in values — a greater appreciation of things that are simple and ordinary. And they are more in touch with themselves — their needs, their aspirations, and their joys. All this is serving the soul, which demands authenticity. And one needn't go through a traumatic experience for this kind of transformation: regular meditation, or quiet time spent alone or in nature, can also help to bring about an "altered" state of consciousness, in which we are more receptive to the voice of the soul.

You may ask if some souls don't come into this world already twisted and troubled, struggling with the accumulated karma of their past. Yes, of course. And this is where wise parents and skilled spiritual helpers are needed. Disturbed children and malfunctioning adults cannot merely be dismissed as delinquents, misfits, oddballs or trouble-makers, nor as innocent victims of a dysfunctional family, a hypocritical society, or imperfect genes. They may indeed be carrying a karmic burden, and they must be helped to understand it, lighten it, and correct it for the next time around. In other words, there is no place either for blame or indulgence, but rather for help and compassion.

Even without massive problems in our lives, it pays to understand where our soul is coming from. Past life channeling can help tremendously with this, but also, if we pay attention to what attracts us and repels us, which situations fill us with joy or fear, even the kind of people we bring into our lives, we can begin to comprehend what our pattern is, and what old hurdles we need to overcome. A lot of the things we call "hang ups" are actually *hang-overs* — memories and habits from former lives that have not yet been resolved and discarded. Many phobias, for example, are based on old memories, which now attach themselves to new situations.

But the soul does not only transmit problems and pain: more importantly, it inspires us and fires our imagination. It is the fertile field of fantasy. When Joseph Campbell said, "Follow your bliss", he was talking about the soul — not the gut, not the brain, and not even the emotions. They simply inform the soul; they do not replace it. And when Shakespeare, through Polonius, says, "To thine own self be true", he was also talking about the soul.

For the soul is the core of our being, and while we may know each other — and ourselves — through our physical appearance and our thoughts and our feelings, it is much harder and rarer to know another's soul. Only to the degree that we open ourselves up, become more brave and more transparent — and, at the same time, more receptive to others — do we begin to see souls and interact at the soul level. Sometimes, great tragedy will cause this to happen, or great joy or great love, with the risk that once the event has passed, we close up again.

But one process in our lives can lead us to soul-awareness, and that is the process of growing older. The awareness may begin at thirty or fifty or seventy, or perhaps — unfortunately — never, but the potential is always there, and it increases with the years. One might even say that with advanced age, as the body grows frailer and the mind less sharp and the emotions more muted, the soul at last has a chance to emerge! Or, as other faculties erode, the soul stands out in high relief. But those explanations are somewhat negative.

It seems truer and better to say that the soul is with us from birth, that it is with us every moment of our lives as both a reminder and a beacon, and depending on how we honor it over our lifetime, it becomes enriched or impoverished. In either case, it becomes more "visible" — to ourselves and to others — for our thoughts and words and deeds have defined it. It has recorded each of our transgressions, regressions, and progressions.

The fearful Judgment Day, when souls are weighed, does not occur *en masse* when the world ends, but when our lives end — each one of us. Then we know how the scales tilt. If we have to shift the balance and have the time to do it — as during a long illness — we may be considered fortunate. There are people who spend the last painful years and months of their lives writing letters and arranging reunions to clear up old misunderstandings, to forgive others and to ask forgiveness. If death comes fast, within minutes or hours, it may mean that karmically the person is ready to go, has done the clearing. Or it may mean that time was wasted, opportunities were not seized, and the work will have to be picked up the next time around.

It is our choice: to drag our soul around like a kitchen mop and shove it into the broom closet of our mind, or to pull it out of the attic like a cherished heirloom, restore it to its proper place, and keep it gleaming.

Chapter 15

CONCLUSION

We grow old more through indolence, than through age.
/ Queen Christina of Sweden

Conclusion? There is never a conclusion when you're talking about life.

There is never a bottom line, never a final statement, never a closing remark. And that's as it should be, because life is full of unexpected twists and turns, and surprises, and opportunities — and dead-ends and detours, too. If you reach a point where you think you finally "understand", and where you seem to have found an operating system that works, beware! It won't last forever. It may be good for a few months or a few years, but a subtle shift or a sudden change in circumstances will cause it to stall, to sputter, even to explode.

We've all experienced this in one way or another: a job that is terminated even though we're still effective at it; a relationship or a marriage that dissolves even though we're still committed to it; a child who gets into trouble in spite of our ongoing love and concern; an accident or an illness that befalls us in spite of our caution and care; a way of life that inexplicably turns sour or barren. Often, these changes occur because something "outside" has changed, and we haven't noticed it. But just as often, the change has occurred within ourselves — and we haven't noticed it. Monotony and boredom have set in, complacency has taken over, there are stirrings of vague discontent. We become deaf and blind to that which is so easy and repetitious. We lose our conscious link to it; it becomes robotized.

When the universe gives us a jolt, it is telling us it's time to make some changes. The old ways are worn out: they aren't working anymore. This is painful, and it's inevitable. But it's a god-given opportunity to take stock and do some thorough house-cleaning.

Of course, we run off to a therapist, call up friends at midnight, and consider going on Prozac. But this should also be a time for serious reflection, for time alone. In physical terms, it is when the hard-driving executive gets a heart attack and is forced to let up on his work. Or when the over-zealous, self-sacrificing mother breaks a leg and is finally forced to rest and be taken care of herself. An emotional/intellectual crisis, though less visible than a physical one, is an equally shrill warning: let go.

And letting go is usually much harder to do than holding on. We cling to the familiar, no matter how hurtful it is, because we fear uncertainty and the unknown. Worse, we fear emptiness. Yet only by creating that emptiness, by clearing away some space, can we make room for something new to come in.

Will it be better? It has to be, for as long as we deliberately and knowingly eradicate what we recognize as having been "bad" or "wrong" or "harmful", we are eliminating the possibility that we will attract — or be lured into — that unhappy situation again. But when we deny what has harmed us, and cling to the memory of it, we are sure to repeat the experience. "Hell is other people", said Sartre, but hell is just as often ourselves — the result of our careless/ dependent/ demanding/ dishonest/ timid/ reactive/ arrogant/ passive/ aggressive/ evasive/ ambivalent behavior and attitudes. And our refusal to change.

The process of unearthing our hidden beliefs and attitudes is a conscious one, best helped by a thoughtful and trusted therapist. But it also calls on our intuition: our memories, our dreams, our associations. When we begin to see the patterns in our life — and there *are* patterns — we can begin to see cause and effect. And it is not always unpleasant. Just reflect: What events have brought you the most happiness, the most satisfaction, the most peace? How much of yourself was invested, what were the efforts you made, and how much just fell into your lap? It isn't surprising that our deepest, most long-lasting joys are not the result of fortuitous events that "fall into our lap", but the fruit of our own labors.

It is important to remember this during those times

when your operating system — your *modus vivendi* — gets stalled or shattered. When luck or Fate or God Herself seems to have abandoned you, when life seems to hold no promise, examine what you've been doing — or not doing — and stop it. Give yourself time to think and dream and mourn and browse, and one day a light will flicker. Follow it, and you may find the new direction, the new goal, and the way to get there.

In fact, a short-cut is to try doing the *opposite* of what you've been doing! If you've been a highly sociable, outgoing person, try being more reserved and reclusive. If you've been leading a quiet, solitary life, push yourself into some social activities. If you're naturally conservative, read or wear or imagine something outrageous. If you're unattached or unaffiliated, try doing some serious charity or community work. This kind of temporary "role-playing" is harmless. It may bore you, annoy you, or eventually fascinate you, but you'll get a bigger, clearer picture of life's potentials and expand your own self-image.

For role-playing of this sort does not imply subterfuge or insincerity. Rather, it is a way to discover different facets of ourselves, like trying on different wardrobes. We are different personalities when we are wearing jeans than when we are wearing evening clothes. We haven't changed our values or our character, but we *have* changed our outlook and behavior. This in turn will change the way others see us and respond to us, and that changes our experience.

Can it be done as we grow older? Of course. It may actually get easier as we get older because we have fewer people depending on us, and fewer social and professional demands.

Another important life-saver and life-extender is friendship. It's a terribly sad truth that as the years go by, we lose our friends to debilitating illness and death. They cannot be replicated, but they must be replaced. Often, they are replaced by people who are very different, or much younger, and this gives us the chance to play new roles, too, in a way that we cannot do with our family, where patterns of relationship have become ingrained. That is why it's important not to spurn new acquaintances: it may be difficult at first to relate to them, but ultimately, they may bring us new and broader experiences.

Perhaps the most obvious thing that I haven't discussed yet is money. Along with health — which I've referred to — having sufficient money to live on is an absolute necessity. There can be no real sense of peace and security, particularly as one grows older, without adequate financial resources. Even if you start late in life, a realistic appraisal of your realistic needs is imperative, and a realistic plan on how to meet them. This may mean continuing to work (which is by no means a bad thing), or doing part-time work, or agreeing to have your spouse work, or simply designing a more economical budget. (Do you really need two cars? Do you really need house seats at the theater? Do you really need a winter cruise?) Scaling-down does not necessarily mean deprivation.

The French have long had a clever way to help aging people supplement their income. It's called *viager*: it allows you to sell your apartment or home to someone, but continue to live in it until your death. The buyer pays you an initial deposit on the property, and then continues to pay a monthly allowance until your death — rather like an annuity. The most famous *viager* case was Jeanne Calment, who outlived her first purchaser and nearly outlived his heirs: she died at 121!

Early planning is crucial to ensuring comfortable later years. But later on, creative solutions can almost always be found. More and more, people are thinking about the possibility of living together in small groups or mini-communes. (They may be the flower children of the '70's!) Extended families, created by divorce and remarriage, might provide other alternatives to living alone: the recombinations offer a bigger pool of "relatives" to choose from! House-sitting or permanent caretaking are other options that might alleviate financial stress.

There are numerous economic, political, cultural, demographic, and social questions related to aging, but one would have to be simply utopian to think all those areas could be explored, analyzed, coordinated and resolved democratically — or even undemocratically — for everyone's good. Pressure can be exerted in certain problem areas where there are gross inequities or injustices (such as taxation and medical insurance). But in the end, solutions for ourselves must be found *by* ourselves, and that all begins within. It may often seem that time works against us, but more often it works *for* us. Time heals, time teaches, time matures us. Time SAGES us, and as we sage, our lives will become richer, happier, and more meaningful.

Growing up and growing out (out-growing) is a process to be enjoyed, and growing older is simply the way we measure that process. What is important is the way we work with it, the way we enhance it. It is up to each of us to make the most of it.

❖

If this book has been meaningful to you, and you would like to share it with friends, additional copies can be ordered directly from the author by e-mail: joanzshore@yahoo.com

Or by regular mail:
        3 Boulevard Henri IV
        Paris 75004
        France

JOUVE
11, bd de Sébastopol, 75001 Paris
Imprimé sur presse rotative numérique
N° 336475R - Dépôt Légal : Novembre 2003

Imprimé en France